# GOLDEN GATE BRIDGE

**Judy Wearing, Tom Riddolls, and Heather Kissock**

www.av2books.com

AV² provides enriched content that supplements and complements this book. Weigl's AV² books strive to create inspired learning and engage young minds in a total learning experience.

## Your AV² Media Enhanced books come alive with...

### Audio
Listen to sections of the book read aloud.

### Key Words
Study vocabulary, and complete a matching word activity.

### Video
Watch informative video clips.

### Quizzes
Test your knowledge.

### Embedded Weblinks
Gain additional information for research.

### Slide Show
View images and captions, and prepare a presentation.

Go to **www.av2books.com**, and enter this book's unique code.

### BOOK CODE

**J48439**

### Try This!
Complete activities and hands-on experiments.

**... and much, much more!**

**AV² by Weigl** brings you media enhanced books that support active learning.

Published by AV² by Weigl
350 5th Avenue, 59th Floor
New York, NY 10118

Website: www.av2books.com    www.weigl.com

Library of Congress Cataloging-in-Publication Data

Wearing, Judy.
  Golden Gate Bridge / Judy Wearing & Tom Riddolls.
    pages cm -- (Virtual field trip)
Includes index.
  Summary: "Explores the history, the people, and the science behind the construction of the Golden Gate Bridge. Intended for fourth to sixth grade students"-- Provided by publisher.
  Audience: Grades 4 to 6.
  ISBN 978-1-62127-463-6 (hardcover : alk. paper) -- ISBN 978-1-62127-469-8 (softcover : alk. paper)
  1.  Golden Gate Bridge (San Francisco, Calif.)--Juvenile literature.  I. Riddolls, Tom. II. Title.
  TG25.S225W429 2014
  624.2'30979461--dc23
                  2012044673

Printed in the United States of America in North Mankato, Minnesota
1 2 3 4 5 6 7 8 9 0  17 16 15 14 13

032013
WEP301112

Editor: Heather Kissock
Design: Terry Paulhus

Every reasonable effort has been made to trace ownership and to obtain permission to reprint copyright material. The publishers would be pleased to have any errors or omissions brought to their attention so that they may be corrected in subsequent printings.

Weigl acknowledges Getty Images as its primary image supplier for this title.

# Contents

# What Is the Golden Gate Bridge?

The Golden Gate Bridge is one of the best-known landmarks in the United States. This **suspension bridge** was built in the 1930s to connect Marin County to the city of San Francisco. Prior to its construction, people had to take a **ferry** across the bay or travel around the entire edge of it to get from one side to the other. That trip was more than 100 miles (161 kilometers) long. Building the bridge reduced that distance to 1.3 miles (2.1 km), and the trip took far less time.

The Golden Gate Bridge faced many challenges before and during its construction. It was built during the Great Depression, a time when the economy was slow and many people were without work. Even though building the bridge would provide people with jobs, it was difficult to raise the money needed for the project. There were also many people who felt that a bridge could not be built across the bay due to its high winds, strong ocean currents, and almost-constant, heavy fog.

At least one person, however, believed that the bridge could be built. An **engineer** named Joseph Strauss drew a plan to build the bridge and gave it to local authorities. In spite of people's concerns, he was given approval to begin the project. It took more than 10 years to organize the construction of the bridge, but it was built in only four years.

When it opened in 1937, the Golden Gate Bridge was the longest suspension bridge in the world. That record stood for 27 years. Today, the bridge is known for its commanding towers, sweeping cables, and colorful orange frame.

# Snapshot of California

California is located on the southern part of the United States' West Coast. The Pacific Ocean makes up the state's western border. California shares its northern border with Oregon. To the east are Nevada and Arizona. Mexico lies to its south.

## INTRODUCING CALIFORNIA

**CAPITAL CITY:** Sacramento

**FLAG:**

**MOTTO:** Eureka

**NICKNAME:** The Golden State

**POPULATION:** 37,691,912 (2011)

**ADMITTED TO THE UNION:** September 9, 1850

**CLIMATE:** Cool, rainy winters and dry summers

**SUMMER TEMPERATURE:** Ranges from of 64° to 116° Fahrenheit (18° to 47° Celsius)

**WINTER TEMPERATURE:** Ranges from of 40° to 73°F (4° to 23°C)

**TIME ZONE:** Pacific Standard Time (PST)

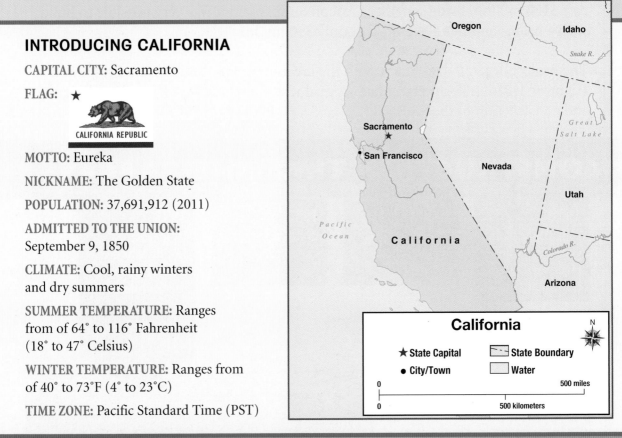

## California Symbols

California has several official symbols. Some symbols represent the features that distinguish the area from other parts of the United States. Others indicate the unique place California has in the history of the country.

**OFFICIAL FLOWER**
California Poppy

**OFFICIAL BIRD**
California Quail

**OFFICIAL TREE**
California Redwood

# A Step Back in Time

San Francisco Bay was a busy place in the early 20<sup>th</sup> century. The ferries that crossed the bay were always bustling, and the ports were often crowded with lineups of cars. People began to ask if it was possible to build a bridge across the open ocean of the Golden Gate. Most bridge engineers said it would be impossible or that it would cost $100 million. Bridge engineer Joseph Strauss said it was very possible to build such a bridge and that it would cost only $30 million.

The project began to take shape with the creation of the Golden Gate Bridge and Highway District. Formed in 1928, its goal was to organize the financing, design, and construction of the bridge.

## CONSTRUCTION TIMELINE

**1928**
The Golden Gate Bridge and Highway District is formed.

**1929**
Joseph Strauss is made chief engineer.

**1932**
Bonds are issued to fund construction.

**1933**
Construction begins. The two **anchorages** and the **foundation** for the north tower are completed.

To help with the construction of the bridge, factories across the country made 83,000 tons (75,296 tonnes) of steel parts and shipped them to San Francisco.

Due to the state of the economy at the time, the Golden Gate Bridge and Highway District found it difficult to raise the funds. In 1930, it asked the district's voters for permission to issue $35 million in **bonds**. Voters risked their houses and farms to provide the **collateral** needed for the bonds. They believed that tolls collected from traffic on the bridge would pay back the money. Over time, they were proven right.

Although Joseph Strauss is credited as the designer of the Golden Gate Bridge, he received a great deal of help from other bridge engineers and designers.

### 1935
The south tower is finished.

### 1936
The main cables and steel structure for the road are ready.

### 1937
The road is added. On May 27th, the Golden Gate Bridge is opened for people to walk across. Vehicles are allowed on the bridge the next day.

### 1938
Joseph Strauss dies of a heart attack not long after the bridge is completed.

A suspension bridge is a kind of "hanging road."

About four million vehicles crossed the Golden Gate Bridge in its first year.

# The Location

The Golden Gate Bridge is located at the mouth of San Francisco Bay. It was named for the water it spans. The mouth of the San Francisco Bay is actually a **strait** called the Golden Gate. Explorer John Charles Frémont gave it this name in 1846. It reminded him of the Golden Horn, a piece of land that forms the harbor of Istanbul in Turkey.

With its graceful curves and tall towers, the Golden Gate Bridge is one of the most spectacular bridges in the country.

# The Golden Gate Bridge Today

The Golden Gate Bridge continues to provide people with easy access between San Francisco and Marin County. About 40 million vehicles cross the Golden Gate Bridge each year. The Golden Gate Bridge is a toll bridge. It costs money for a vehicle to take the trip across.

**Weight** The entire bridge weighs 60,000 tons (54,431 tonnes).

**Height** The towers stretch 746 feet (227 m) above the water. The **deck** is 220 feet (67 m) above the water.

746 feet (227 m)

8,981 feet (2,737 m)

**Length** The bridge is 8,981 feet (2,737 m) long in total. The longest span, from the north to south tower, is 4,200 feet (1,280 m) long.

220 feet (67 m)

# The Structure of the Bridge

*When planning the Golden Gate Bridge, Joseph Strauss and his team wanted the bridge to be grand in appearance but strong enough to withstand its physical environment. Building a suspension bridge met both of these requirements.*

Due to its unique harp-like design, when the bridge opened in 1937, the *San Francisco Chronicle* referred to it as a "thirty-five million dollar steel harp."

**Art Deco**  Like many structures of this era, the Golden Gate Bridge is designed in the art deco style. This is a type of design known for its geometric patterns, bright colors, and elegant, curving surfaces. These features are found throughout the bridge, from its majestic towers to its sweeping cables.

The rectangular holes in the towers decrease in size as they ascend the tower. This helps emphasize the height of the towers.

**Towers**  The Golden Gate Bridge has two main towers that rise from the waters to support the bridge's main cables. Rectangular openings run up the height of each tower, giving the bridge a light, airy appearance. Wide, upright ribbing on each tower's horizontal **struts** gives the bridge texture when sunlight shines on it.

Suspender cables run vertically from the main cables to the deck. They support the weight of the deck and its traffic.

**Cables**  The bridge's two main cables pass over the towers where they are held in place by large steel casings called saddles. The cables are secured to the ground in anchorages found on each side of the bridge. About 80,000 miles (128,748 km) of cable was used to make the main cables. Each cable is 7,650 feet (2,332 m) long and is made up of approximately 27,500 individual wires.

**Deck** The deck is the busiest part of the Golden Gate Bridge. The bridge's roadway and its sidewalks run along the top of the deck. It is via the deck that people get from one side of the strait to the other. The bridge has sidewalks on each side of the bridge for pedestrians and cyclists.

About 112,000 vehicles travel the six-lane highway every day.

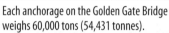

Each anchorage on the Golden Gate Bridge weighs 60,000 tons (54,431 tonnes).

**Anchorages** The Golden Gate Bridge's anchorages are located at each end of the bridge. These massive reinforced concrete blocks are set into and connected to the underlying rock on each side of the bridge. Inside the anchorage, the cable is unwound and spread out to strengthen its grip to the concrete. The anchorages serve to **ground** the bridge and keep it stable.

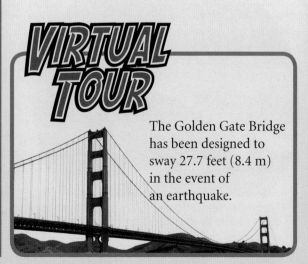

### VIRTUAL TOUR

The Golden Gate Bridge has been designed to sway 27.7 feet (8.4 m) in the event of an earthquake.

# Features of the Bridge

*The Golden Gate Bridge is both attractive and useful. It has several features that ensure the safety of its users. It also has places that provide visitors with the opportunity to learn about the history of the bridge and its builders.*

**Paint** The Golden Gate Bridge's orange paint provides a splash of color that is part of the bridge's art deco style. It also protects the bridge from the humidity and saltwater that surround it. The paint covers the metal and helps to keep the humidity and salt from eating away at the steel.

The official name for the color of the paint used on the Golden Gate Bridge is International Orange.

There are few lights at the top of the towers. This was done so that the towers would appear to disappear into the night sky.

**Lights** Lighting helps to guide people and vehicles over and around the bridge. A series of art deco lamp posts run along the length of the deck. Eight lights on each of the bridge's main cables, as well as a series of floodlights on the towers, help showcase the structure's shape at night. Beacons at the top of each tower flash red to warn aircraft of the bridge's location. Beacons found lower on the tower piers flash light out to sea to let ships know how close they are to the bridge.

## Strauss Statue

Within the Strauss Plaza stands a bronze statue of Joseph Strauss. Created by sculptor Frederick William Schweigardt, the statue was unveiled in 1941 and sat near the roadway for a number of years. It was eventually moved to its current location in the gardens of the plaza.

A plaque at the base of the statue pays tribute to Strauss's role in the construction of the Golden Gate Bridge.

## Strauss Plaza

The bridge's visitor area, called Strauss Plaza, is located at the south end of the bridge. The Bridge Pavilion serves as the visitors' center, providing information about the structure and its history. The plaza also features a gift shop, a restaurant, and gardens leading to excellent views of the bridge itself.

The Bridge Pavilion is painted International Orange to complement the bridge itself.

## Foghorns

Fog is a constant in the San Francisco area. To ensure that ships know where the bridge is when visibility is poor, the bridge has a set of foghorns that can be sounded when needed. The foghorns are located in two places. One set is found in the middle of the bridge, and the other is at the bridge's south end.

The summer months are San Francisco's foggiest time of year. Foghorns may be sounded for more than five hours a day when heavy fog rolls in.

# Big Ideas behind the Bridge

A bridge must support its own weight as well as the weight of any objects or people that travel over it. The materials used to make the bridge, as well as the bridge's design, must all work together to create a strong structure. The Golden Gate Bridge's strength allows it to withstand high winds and fast-moving waters, and to hold the traffic that crosses it each day.

Both the towers and the anchorages are built into the ground. The bridge's cables work to transfer the weight of the bridge and its traffic away from the structure itself.

## Suspension

Suspension bridges work due to the forces of **compression** and **tension**. These forces transfer the weight of the bridge and its traffic to other points. The Golden Gate Bridge's roadway hangs from cables that stretch across the bridge's entire span. The towers help to support the roadway's weight. Compression presses down on the roadway, but the cables counter this pressure by pushing it up the towers and down into the ground. The bridge stays stable as a result. The forces of tension are handled by the supporting cables, which are attached to anchorages. The weight of the bridge and its traffic stretch the cables tight, causing tension. This tension is relayed to the anchorages and into the ground, taking the pressure off the bridge itself and keeping it firmly in place.

## Trusses

Due to their length and use of cables, suspension bridges are exposed to a force called torsion. This is a twisting force normally caused by high winds. If not controlled, it can seriously damage a bridge. On the Golden Gate Bridge, this force is combatted through the use of trusses. A truss is a type of framework made up of metal or wood that gives a structure **rigidity**. The trusses on the Golden Gate Bridge reinforce the bridge's deck. This makes it more resistant to twisting forces and helps to keep the bridge from collapsing due to twisting movements during earthquakes.

In recent years, the bridge's trusses have been refitted with newer, stronger materials.

# Science at Work at the Golden Gate Bridge

Building the Golden Gate Bridge required planning, labor, and the best technology available at the time. In the case of the Golden Gate Bridge, the construction machines used were a combination of new and old technology.

## Spinning the Cable

Running the cables from one end of the bridge to the other was a time-consuming task. First, the wires were bound around giant spools attached to the bridge's anchorages. One end of the wire was tied to the anchorage, while the rest of the wire was wound around the giant wheel. This wheel was then pushed across the bridge, with the cable unwinding as the wheel rolled. Once the wheel reached the other side of the bridge, the cable was attached to that side's anchorage, and the process began again. To speed up the work, two wheels were used at the same time. Each started at opposite ends of the bridge and passed by each other in the center.

## Rivets

There are more than one million steel rivets holding the Golden Gate Bridge together. A rivet is a short shaft of metal with a rounded head at one end. When two pieces of steel are joined, a hole is drilled through both. The shaft of the rivet is put through the hole and is then hit with a hammer. The hammer spreads the end of the rivet. This makes one end of the rivet wider, holding the two pieces of metal in place.

Rivets hold the bridge's steel pieces together.

The Golden Gate Bridge uses the longest bridge cables ever made. They could circle Earth three times.

**VIRTUAL TOUR**

There are 600,000 rivets in each tower to hold the steel pieces together. Each rivet was tightened by hand.

# The Builders

The Great Depression was a time when many people did not have jobs. The construction of the Golden Gate Bridge provided jobs to people of various backgrounds. Farmers and office clerks became steelworkers. Cement workers built the anchorages. Engineers planned, designed, and managed the construction process.

### Joseph Strauss Engineer

Joseph Baermann Strauss was born in Cincinnati, Ohio, on January 9, 1870. After completing high school, Strauss attended the University of Cincinnati. He graduated in 1892 with a degree in commerce.

Strauss's fascination with bridges came as a result of a hospital stay while attending university. The view from his hospital room was of the Cincinnati-Covington Bridge, one of America's first suspension bridges. This bridge inspired him to become a bridge engineer, and he soon joined the engineering firm of Ralph Modjeski, a well-known bridge engineer.

While there, Strauss became interested in designing moveable bridges. He invented two types of bridge. One was a type of **bascule drawbridge**, which uses **counterweights** to balance the moveable parts. The other was a type of vertical-lift bridge. On this type of bridge, the moveable part is lifted straight up from the rest of the bridge in a horizontal position.

Strauss eventually left Modjeski's firm to form his own company. Bascule bridges were the company's specialty, and it built 400 of these bridges across North America. However, they were fairly small in size. Joseph had always dreamed of building a big bridge. When he heard about the Golden Gate Bridge project, he saw an opportunity to achieve this goal. He fought for more than 10 years to make the bridge a reality.

The effort it took to build the Golden Gate Bridge tired Strauss. He died in Los Angeles, California, on May 16, 1938, one year after the bridge was completed.

## Structural Engineers

Structural engineers make sure structures are safe, strong, and stable. They ensure that the bridge's design and construction materials will survive the pressures of the bridge's environment. In the case of the Golden Gate Bridge, this includes strong water currents, high winds, and potential earthquakes. Structural engineering requires strong technical knowledge and a solid understanding of the scientific principles involved in construction processes. Most structural engineers have at least a bachelor's degree in engineering.

Structural engineers inspected the bridge throughout its construction to ensure that it was going to be safe for the traffic it would handle.

Due to the amount of steel involved, steelworkers were key to the construction of the bridge.

## Steelworkers

Steel makes up a good part of the Golden Gate Bridge. Steelworkers put the metal pieces together. They read the engineer's blueprints, and then put the bridge's framework together. This involved welding or bolting the correct pieces in place. Steelworkers continue to work on the Golden Gate Bridge. They need to be in good physical condition and have strong mechanical skills. Steelworkers should be able to use a variety of tools to inspect the bridge parts and replace any that are worn.

## Cement Masons

Cement masons specialize in handling cement and concrete. They pour wet concrete into molds and make sure it spreads to the necessary thickness. They then level and smooth the surfaces and edges of the cement. Throughout the process, cement masons check how the wind and temperature are affecting the concrete and fix any potential problems. Working with cement is very physical work. Cement masons often kneel and bend over the surface they are working on. They also carry heavy bags of cement. This requires a great deal of physical strength.

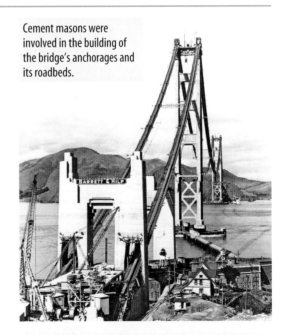
Cement masons were involved in the building of the bridge's anchorages and its roadbeds.

# Similar Structures around the World

Suspension bridges have been used for a very long time. Ancient peoples, such as the Incas, built bridges suspended by cables. With their elegant appearance, suspension bridges often become important landmarks for the places where they reside.

## Akashi Kaikyo Bridge

**BUILT:** 1998
**LOCATION:** Kobe and Awaji-shima, Japan
**DESIGN:** Honshu-Shikoku Bridge Authority
**DESCRIPTION:** Also known as the Pearl Bridge, the Akashi Kaikyo Bridge is now the longest suspension bridge in the world. It is 12,828 feet (3,910 m) long, with towers that are 928 feet (283 m) tall. This bridge is built to stand up to strong winds, tsunamis, and earthquakes.

After the Inca Suspension Bridge has received its annual maintenance, tourists can pay a small fee to cross it.

When first built, the Akashi Kaikyo Bridge was shorter than it is today. An earthquake in 1995 stretched the bridge another 3 feet (1 m).

## Inca Suspension Bridge

**BUILT:** 16th century to present
**LOCATION:** Huinchiri, Peru
**DESIGN:** Incas
**DESCRIPTION:** Known as the last Inca hanging bridge, this bridge extends across the Apurimac River. It is made from stiff grasses woven into a strong, thick rope that is 150 feet (46 m) long. Villagers from both sides of the river come together for three days every year to make new rope for it. They do this to honor their past.

## Brooklyn Bridge

**BUILT:** 1883
**LOCATION:** Manhattan and Brooklyn, New York, United States
**DESIGN:** John Roebling
**DESCRIPTION:** The Brooklyn Bridge joins Brooklyn to New York City. It spans 1,595 feet (486 m) and is the second-busiest bridge in New York City. During its construction, John Roebling died. His son, Washington, took over the project but became ill. His wife helped him complete the bridge.

When the Brooklyn Bridge opened in 1883, it was the longest suspension bridge in the world.

Union Bridge was the first suspension bridge built for vehicle use in Great Britain.

## Union Bridge

**BUILT:** 1820
**LOCATION:** Horncliffe, United Kingdom
**DESIGN:** Captain Samuel Brown
**DESCRIPTION:** One lane of traffic travels 449 feet (137 m) over the River Tweed on the Union Bridge. As the oldest suspension bridge still in use in the United Kingdom, it is protected as an ancient monument. This means that it is considered to be a structure of national importance and, as a result, cannot be changed in any way without special permission.

# Issues Facing the Bridge

Keeping the Golden Gate Bridge in good condition is a year-round job. Its proximity to the ocean brings the bridge in contact with many elements that can have an adverse effect on it. The strong possibility of earthquakes also presents a danger to the structure.

## WHAT IS THE ISSUE?

The environment can work against the bridge. Tides, winds, salty sea water, and humidity all damage the bridge.

San Francisco Bay lies in a region where two **tectonic plates** meet.

## EFFECTS

Strong tides crash against underwater supports, and forceful winds can cause the bridge to sway. Over time, this can weaken the structure. Saltwater and humidity combine to **corrode** the bridge's metal supports.

When tectonic plates move against each other, an earthquake can occur. San Francisco is under a constant threat of earthquakes.

## ACTION TAKEN

People constantly monitor the condition of the bridge. Rivets are replaced when necessary, and protective paint is reapplied when chipped. The bridge has had extensive renovations to fix salt and humidity damage.

In 1997, the bridge began an extensive renovation to make it more resistant to earthquakes. Foundations and trusses were strengthened. Towers and braces were replaced. New parts were also added to help it adjust to the shifting an earthquake can cause.

# Build a Suspension Bridge

A suspension bridge has five main parts. These are towers, anchorages, main cables, suspending cables, and a deck. Try building a model suspension bridge using materials you may have around the house.

## Materials

- 6 paper tower rolls pizza box
- glue
- long pipe cleaners
- scissors

- cardboard
- toy car
- corrugated cardboard
- pen or pencil

## Instructions

1. Cut two of the paper towel rolls in half. The full cardboard rolls will be your bridge's towers, and the half-rolls will be its anchorages.

2. Glue the towers to the center of the pizza box. Then, glue two anchorages to each edge of the box. Let the glue dry.

3. Cut small slits into the tops of the towers and anchorages. To begin making the bridge's cable, knot the end of a pipe cleaner. Put the knotted end into one of the slits. Link other pipe cleaners end to end to make the cable longer. String the pipe cleaners from one set of anchorages to the two sets of towers and then to the other set of anchorages.

4. To make the bridge deck, measure the width and length of the bridge. Draw these measurements onto a piece of corrugated cardboard, and then cut out the shape.

5. To suspend the bridge's deck, take several pipe cleaners and bend their tips around the bridge's main cables. Make sure the pipe cleaners extend along the length of the entire bridge, from anchorage to anchorage. Pass these pipe cleaners under the deck and then attach them to the cables on the other side of the bridge. If you need more length, twist more pipe cleaners together. When complete, adjust the pipe cleaners until the deck hangs parallel to the base.

6. How much weight does your bridge hold? Try running a toy car across it. Does the bridge hold the weight of the car? If not, how could you make your bridge stronger?

# Golden Gate Bridge Quiz

**Q** Was the Golden Gate the first suspension bridge in the world?

**A** No. Suspension bridges, in some form, have been around for centuries. Ancient cultures, such as the Incas, were known to have built suspension bridges.

**Q** What is the name of the Golden Gate Bridge's design style?

**A** The bridge was designed using the Art Deco style. This was a popular design style in the 1920s.

**Q** What are the two main forces suspension bridges rely on?

**A** Suspension bridges work as a result of the forces of compression and tension. These forces support the weight of the bridge and its traffic by diverting the pressure to other points.

**Q** Did Joseph Strauss design the bridge by himself?

**A** No. Many engineers and designers helped Joseph Strauss plan the Golden Gate Bridge.

# Key Words

**anchorages:** structures used to hold something else firmly in place

**bascule drawbridge:** a bridge that opens to allow boats to pass through; uses a heavy counterweight to help open and close the bridge

**bonds:** certificates of debt issued in order to raise funds

**collateral:** security pledged for the repayment of a loan

**compression:** the act of being flattened or squeezed together by pressure

**corrode:** a process in which an object is worn away by a chemical action

**counterweights:** objects that balance opposing forces

**deck:** a platform on which bridge traffic travels

**engineer:** someone who applies scientific principles to the design of structures

**ferry:** a boat used to carry people and vehicles across water

**foundation:** the part of a structure that helps support its weight

**ground:** fix firmly on a foundation

**rigidity:** stiffness

**strait:** a narrow passage of water that links two larger bodies of water

**struts:** the bracing pieces of a structure's framework

**suspension bridge:** a bridge that has a deck supported by cables anchored at both ends

**tectonic plates:** pieces of Earth's surface that are constantly moving

**tension:** the state of being stretched

# Index

# Log on to www.av2books.com

AV² by Weigl brings you media enhanced books that support active learning. Go to www.av2books.com, and enter the special code found on page 2 of this book. You will gain access to enriched and enhanced content that supplements and complements this book. Content includes video, audio, weblinks, quizzes, a slide show, and activities.

## AV² Online Navigation

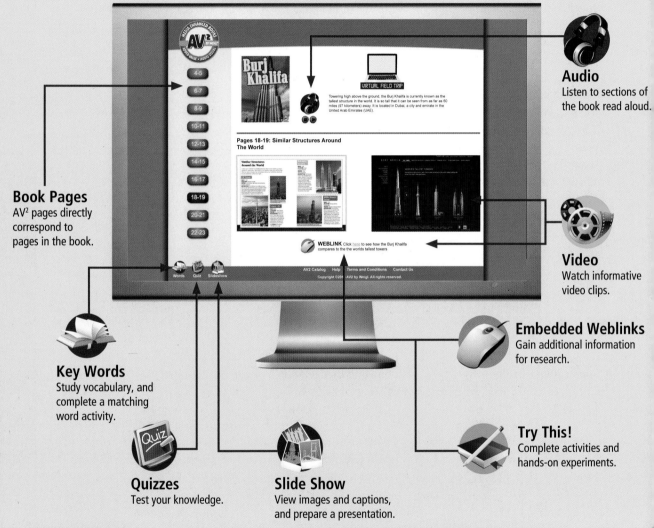

**Audio**
Listen to sections of the book read aloud.

**Book Pages**
AV² pages directly correspond to pages in the book.

**Video**
Watch informative video clips.

**Key Words**
Study vocabulary, and complete a matching word activity.

**Embedded Weblinks**
Gain additional information for research.

**Quizzes**
Test your knowledge.

**Slide Show**
View images and captions, and prepare a presentation.

**Try This!**
Complete activities and hands-on experiments.

AV² was built to bridge the gap between print and digital. We encourage you to tell us what you like and what you want to see in the future.

## Sign up to be an AV² Ambassador at www.av2books.com/ambassador.